Narrator: **Chuck Riley**

Featuring the voice talents of:

C-3PO: **Anthony Daniels**
Princess Leia: **Pat Parris**
Darth Vader: **Brock Peters**
Uncle Owen: **Charles Howerton**
Luke Skywalker: **Joshua Fardon**
Obi-Wan Kenobi: **Roy Dotrice**
Han Solo: **Perry King**
Jabba the Hutt: **Randy Thornton**
Grand Moff Tarkin: **Tony Pope**

Illustrated by **Brian Rood**

Music composed by John Williams
Read-Along produced by Randy Thornton
Read-Along executive produced by Ted Kryczko
Recording engineer: Jeff Sheridan
Adapted by Randy Thornton

All music published by Bantha Music (BMI), co-published by Warner-Tamerlane Publishing Corp. (BMI)

℗ 2015 Walt Disney Disney Records/Lucasfilm Ltd. © & TM 2015 Lucasfilm Ltd.
All rights reserved.

EPISODE IV
A NEW HOPE
Read-Along
STORYBOOK AND CD

Hello. I am C-3PO, and you are about to listen to the story of Star Wars: A New Hope.

You can also read along with the story in your book. Unless you are already programmed to know when the pages end, you will know it is time to turn the page when you hear this sound....

I believe the storyteller is ready, so let us begin.

A long time ago in a galaxy far, far away....

© & TM 2015 Lucasfilm Ltd. All rights reserved. Published by Disney • Lucasfilm Press, an imprint of Disney Book Group. No part of this book may be reproduced or transmitted in any form or by any means, electronic or mechanical, including photocopying, recording, or by any information storage and retrieval system, without written permission from the publisher. For information address Disney • Lucasfilm Press, 1101 Flower Street, Glendale, California 91201.

Printed in the United States of America
First Paperback Edition, February 2015
First Hardcover Edition, February 2015
1 3 5 7 9 10 8 6 4 2
ISBN 978-1-4847-2664-8
G942-9090-6-15008

Los Angeles • New York

THERE WAS A PERIOD OF CIVIL WAR. Rebel spaceships fighting for freedom had won their first victory against the evil Galactic Empire. During the battle, rebel spies managed to steal secret design plans to the Empire's ultimate weapon, the Death Star—an armored space station with enough power to destroy an entire planet. Pursued by the Empire's agents, Princess Leia of Alderaan raced home aboard her rebel starship, carrying the plans that could save her people.

Suddenly, a laser blast rocked Princess Leia's starship. Inside, two droids—C-3PO and R2-D2—tried to steady themselves. The larger of the two, C-3PO, turned to his small counterpart, R2-D2. "We'll be destroyed for sure. This is madness!"

The starship began to shake, straining against an invisible force. It was caught in the tractor beam of an Imperial Star Destroyer, and was being pulled into a docking bay.

In a burst of flame, the hatch to the rebel starship was opened and Imperial stormtroopers poured in, firing in every direction. The rebel soldiers were quickly overtaken.

A massive black-cloaked figure stepped through the charred doorway. It was the Dark Lord of the Sith. The feared Darth Vader.

In another part of the ship, C-3PO was looking for R2-D2, whom he'd lost during the attack. Following the familiar sound of his friend, C-3PO came across a beautiful woman kneeling in front of the little droid. She turned and quickly slipped into the shadows.

"There you are. Where have you been? Mission? What mission?" C-3PO followed the little droid as he entered an escape pod.

"I'm going to regret this." The pod burst from the ship and headed for Tatooine, the planet below.

Within moments, Princess Leia was captured and brought before the Dark Lord. "Darth Vader. Only you could be so bold."

"Don't act so surprised, Your Highness. You weren't on any mercy mission this time. Several transmissions were beamed to this ship by rebel spies. I want to know what happened to the plans they sent you."

"I'm a member of the Imperial Senate on a diplomatic mission to Alderaan—"

"You are part of the Rebel Alliance and a traitor. Take her away!"

On the desert planet of Tatooine, C-3PO and R2-D2's escape pod had landed. No sooner had they disembarked than they were captured by the Jawas, a group of little hooded creatures. "We're doomed. Do you think they'll melt us down?"

Scavengers by nature, the Jawas claimed the droids as their own and sold them to Owen Lars, a moisture farmer and guardian of Luke Skywalker. "Luke, take these two over to the garage, will you? I want you to have both of these cleaned up before dinner."

As C-3PO was lowered into an oil bath, Luke began to clean the little R2 unit. "You got a lot of carbon scoring here. It looks like you boys have seen a lot of action."

"With all we've been through, sometimes I'm amazed we're in as good condition as we are, what with the Rebellion and all."

"You know of the Rebellion against the Empire?"

"That's how we came to be in your service, if you take my meaning, sir."

Excited by this link to the Rebellion, Luke turned back to R2-D2 and discovered an object in his head rotation joint. "Well, my little friend, you've got something jammed in here real good. Were you on a starcruiser or a—"

There was a flash of light, and suddenly R2-D2 began projecting a holographic image of Princess Leia into the center of the room. "Help me, Obi-Wan Kenobi. You're my only hope."

Luke sat there, dazzled. "Who is she? She's beautiful."

The stubborn R2 unit refused to play back the entire message.

C-3PO interpreted the little droid's mechanical beeps for Luke.

"He says that he's the property of Obi-Wan Kenobi, a resident of these parts. And it's a private message for him."

"I wonder if he means old Ben Kenobi."

"I beg your pardon, sir, but do you know what he's talking about?"

"Well, I don't know anyone named Obi-Wan, but old Ben lives out beyond the Dune Sea. He's kind of a strange old hermit."

Fearing that the droids may have been stolen, Luke set off to deliver them to Ben Kenobi, along with the secret message.

Luke presented Ben with the droids. "I saw part of a message R2-D2 was—"

"I seem to have found it."

"General Kenobi, years ago you served my father in the Clone Wars. Now he begs you to help him in his struggle against the Empire. I have placed information vital to the survival of the Rebellion into the memory systems of this R2 unit. You must see this droid safely delivered to him on Alderaan. This is our most desperate hour. Help me, Obi-Wan Kenobi. You're my only hope."

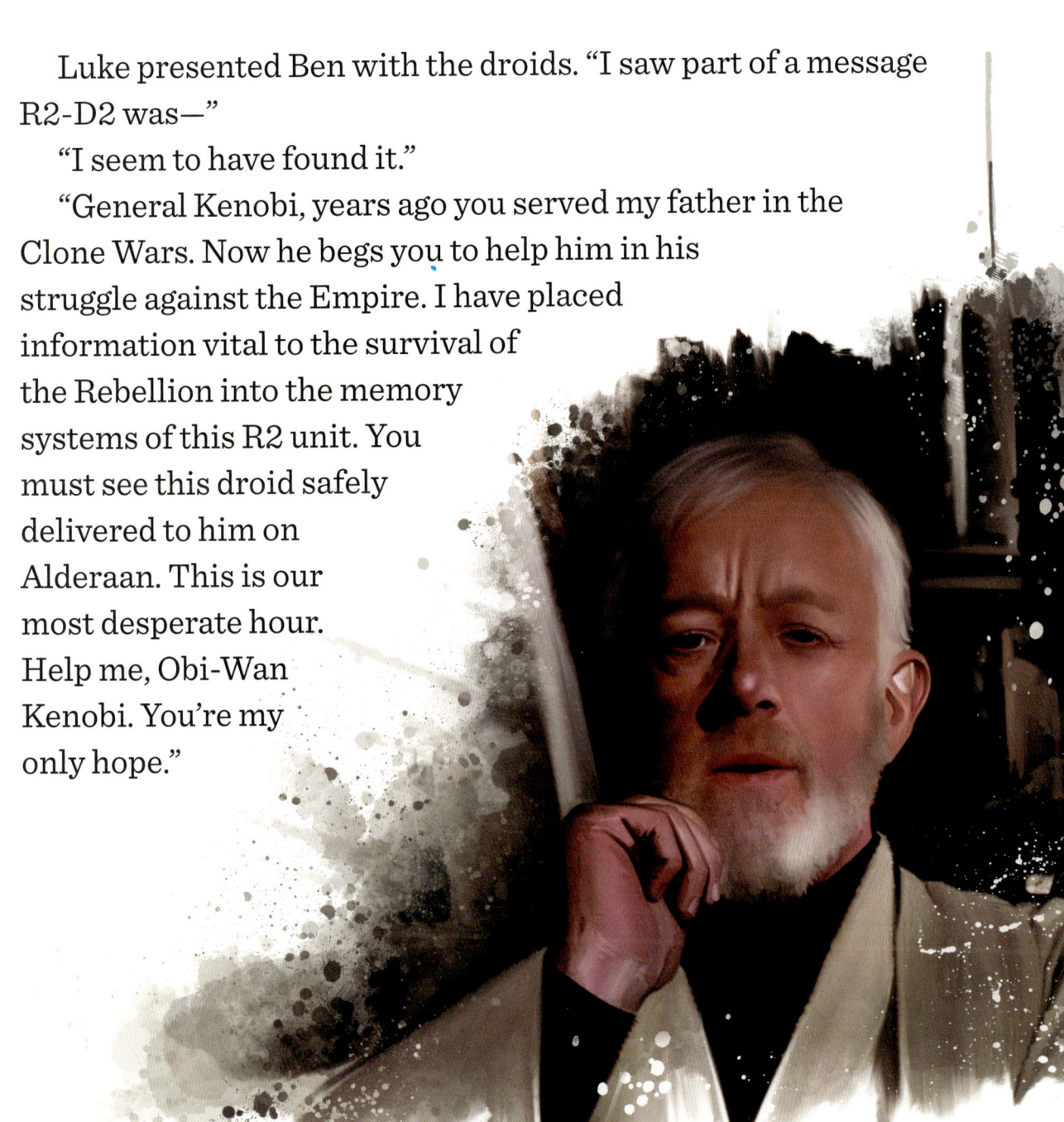

Ben turned to Luke. "I was once a Jedi Knight, like your father."
"My father was a Jedi?"
"Yes . . . and this was his lightsaber." Ben handed Luke the sword. "He wanted you to have it when you were old enough. You should learn the ways of the Force if you're to come with me to Alderaan."
"I can't leave here. I'll take you as far as Anchorhead."
"You must do what you feel is right, of course."

On their way to Anchorhead, Luke, Ben, and the droids came across the Jawa sandcrawler, destroyed by Imperial troops.

"If they traced the robots here, they may have learned who they sold them to. And that would lead them back . . . home!"

"Wait, Luke. It's too dangerous."

But Luke was already in his landspeeder and gone. When he arrived at the farm, he was devastated to find all that he had ever known destroyed and smoldering.

Sadly, he returned to Ben. "I want to come with you to Alderaan. There's nothing here for me now. I want to learn the ways of the Force and become a Jedi like my father."

Though their destination was clear, they still needed a ship and a pilot to take them there. The best place to find a pilot was the Mos Eisley Cantina, home to a strange assortment of creatures from throughout the galaxy. Ben took Luke around and made some introductions.

"Chewbacca here. He's first mate on a ship that might suit us."

The tall Wookiee led them to a table off in the corner where they met a rough-looking star pilot. "Han Solo. I'm the captain of the *Millennium Falcon*. You guys got yourself a ship. We'll leave as soon as you're ready. Docking Bay ninety four."

While Luke and Ben set off to sell the landspeeder for some extra money, Han returned to his ship only to be met by the hideous gangster Jabba the Hut. The vicious Hutt demanded the money that Han owed him. The captain tried to gain some time. "I got a nice easy charter now. Pay you back plus a little extra."

Jabba agreed but he made it clear that if Han failed again, he would put such a high price on his head that he wouldn't be able to go anywhere without an army of bounty hunters waiting to collect it.

The *Millennium Falcon* took off, racing toward Alderaan. Meanwhile, at Alderaan, the Death Star had just entered orbit. On board, Darth Vader was taking the princess to the commander of the space station.

"Princess Leia, before your execution, I would like you to be my first guest at a ceremony that will make this battle station fully operational. No star system will dare oppose the Emperor now."

He turned to the technician. "You may fire when ready." A beam of light shot out of the Death Star, and the planet Alderaan exploded in a tremendous fireball.

At the same moment, the *Millennium Falcon* came out of hyperspace and was suddenly pelted with debris from the destroyed planet. The only thing seemingly intact was a small moon nearby.

"That's no moon. That's a space station." Ben was right.

Suddenly the ship shook violently. Han grabbed the controls. "We're caught in a tractor beam! They're pulling us in!"

When the *Falcon* docked, the Imperial search crew jumped on board. But they found the ship empty. Shaking their heads in disbelief, they left. Han—along with the others—emerged from secret compartments, and climbed aboard the Death Star.

While Ben set off to deactivate the tractor beam, R2 plugged into a Death Star computer and discovered that Princess Leia was aboard. Luke persuaded Han and Chewbacca to help him rescue her. They knocked out some guards, took their uniforms, and disguised themselves as stormtroopers escorting their prisoner, Chewbacca.

Once inside the detention block, they located Leia's cell. She was startled as her door opened and an unusual stormtrooper entered.

"I'm Luke Skywalker. I'm here to rescue you. I've got your R2 unit. I'm here with Ben Kenobi."

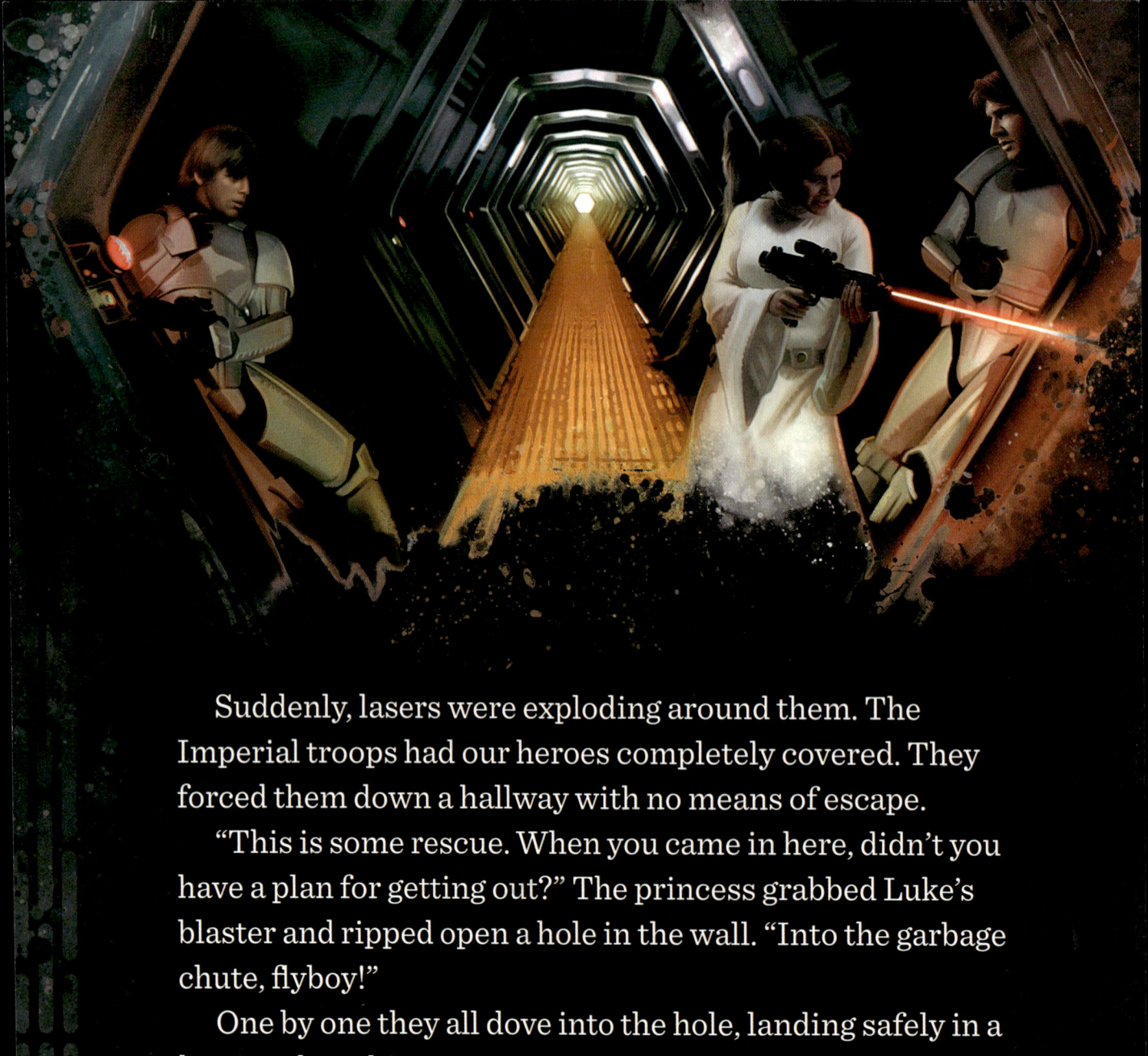

Suddenly, lasers were exploding around them. The Imperial troops had our heroes completely covered. They forced them down a hallway with no means of escape.

"This is some rescue. When you came in here, didn't you have a plan for getting out?" The princess grabbed Luke's blaster and ripped open a hole in the wall. "Into the garbage chute, flyboy!"

One by one they all dove into the hole, landing safely in a huge garbage bin.

Without warning, the walls began to close in on them. They'd landed in a trash compactor! It took all their strength to keep the four sides from crushing them, and for a while it didn't look good.

Then Luke suddenly remembered the droids. He contacted them on his comlink, and instructed R2 to shut down all the garbage mashers. Everyone escaped with barely a scratch.

Meanwhile, Ben had deactivated the tractor beam. Stealthily, the old Jedi made his way back through the hallways to the *Falcon*, when suddenly he felt the presence of the Dark Lord.

"I've been waiting for you, Obi-Wan. We meet again at last. When I left you, I was but the learner; now I am the master." On went his lightsaber.

Ben quickly ignited his sword, too. "Only a master of evil, Darth. You can't win. If you strike me down, I shall become more powerful than you can possibly imagine."

Luke and his friends arrived at the docking bay, where the *Falcon* was in sight. But there was a strange commotion going on at one end, and a group of stormtroopers were watching it closely. It was the battle between the Dark Lord and Obi-Wan Kenobi. Vader would swing and Ben would block.

But when the old Jedi saw Luke, a serene look came over him. He stopped fighting, closed his eyes, and raised his sword to his face. Vader swept his lightsaber through Obi-Wan's cloak, but suddenly he was gone. Only his robes, in a crumpled heap, remained.

Luke was horrified. "NO!"

The stormtroopers spun around and opened fire. Leia and the droids raced to the ship as Han, Chewbacca, and Luke fired back.

Within seconds, the *Millennium Falcon* shot out of the docking bay. But it was not alone. Four Imperial TIE fighters were hot on its trail. Han showed Luke the gunports. "Come on, buddy, we're not out of this yet."

The attack was severe, but our young heroes won. Afterward, they arrived at Rebel Headquarters with the Death Star plans.

But Darth Vader had placed a homing beacon aboard the *Millennium Falcon,* and the Imperial Death Star was approaching. Using the secret plan, the rebels launched their ships and headed straight for the Death Star.

They zoomed across the surface of the space station as enemy laser cannons fired back. It soon became obvious that the Imperial troops had to fight the rebels ship-to-ship. Waves of TIE fighters screamed out of the Death Star and attacked. Even Darth Vader himself manned a fighter.

The Empire was gaining ground. One rebel pilot had failed to hit the weak spot of the space station. Now it was up to Luke. But Vader was right on Luke's heels. "The Force is strong with this one." As Vader was about to fire, a lasershot ripped past him and hit his wingman. The explosion sent Vader's ship spinning into space.

"Yahoo! You're clear, kid. Let's blow this thing and go home." It was Han!

As Luke raced to hit the target, he heard Ben's voice. "Use the Force, Luke." Luke fired two proton torpedoes at the Death Star. It was a direct hit. The rebel ships raced into hyperspace just as the space station exploded in a tremendous flash.

With the destruction of the Death Star, the rebels had won one of their great victories over the Empire. Hundreds of rebel troops gathered together to honor Han Solo and Luke Skywalker for their heroic deeds during the battle. Princess Leia awarded the two men with medals of valor as the crowd cheered their triumph. Through the happiness, however, the rebels knew that, though the dreaded Death Star had been destroyed, the Empire, the Emperor, and Darth Vader were still in power and a threat to freedom. But all that would have to wait until the next adventure . . .